Speak Up

Book 2

Listening and Pronunciation for High Beginning Students

Cheryl Pavlik

Anna Stumpfhauser de Hernandez

Universidad Michoacana de San Nicolás de Hidalgo, Mexico

Heinle & Heinle Publishers

I(T)P An International Thomson Publishing Company

Pacific Grove • Albany • Bonn • Boston • Cincinnati • Detroit • London • Madrid • Melbourne
Mexico City • New York • Paris • San Francisco • Tokyo • Toronto • Washington

The Publication of *Speak Up—Book 2, Second Edition* was directed by the members of the Newbury House Publishing Team at Heinle & Heinle:

Erik Gundersen, *Editorial Director*
John F. McHugh, *Market Development Director*
Kristin Thalheimer, *Production Services Coordinator*
Elizabeth Holthaus, *Team Leader and Director of Production*

Also participating in the publication of this program were:

Publisher: Stanley J. Galek
Project Manager: Linda Lee
Assistant Editor: Karen P. Hazar
Associate Production Editor: Maryellen Eschmann
Manufacturing Coordinator: Mary Beth Hennebury
Photo Researcher: Philippe Heckly
Photo Specialist: Jonathan Stark
Interior Designer: Carol H. Rose
Illustrator: Bob Holmes
Cover Artist and Designer: Kim Wedlake

LIBRARY OF CONGRESS CATALOGING-IN PUBLICATION DATA

Pavlik, Cheryl, 1949-
    Speak up / Cheryl Pavlik
       p.   cm.
    Contents: bk. 1. Listening and pronunciation for beginning
students — bk. 2. Listening and pronunciation for high beginning
students.
    ISBN 0-8384-4996-4 (v. 1.). — ISBN 0-8384-4998-0 (v. 2.)
    1. English language — Textbooks for foreign speakers. 2. English
language — Pronunciation — Problems, exercises, etc.
3. Listening Pronunciation — Problems, exercises, etc. I. Title.
PE1128.P377 1995
428.3'4—dc20
                                        94–25204
                                           CIP

Heinle & Heinle Publishers/A Division of International Thomson Publishing, Inc.

Manufactured in the United States of America
ISBN 0-8384-4998-0

10 9 8 7 6 5 4

Table of Contents

To the Teacher

Speak Up is a comprehensive two-level oral/aural skills program for beginning and high beginning students of English as a second or foreign language (ESL/EFL). Book 1 is designed for beginning level students, Book 2 for high beginners. *Speak Up* presents engaging and relevant contexts that provide students ample opportunity to develop their pronunciation, listening comprehension, and speaking skills.

Since *Speak Up Book 2* is designed for students at a high beginning level, every effort has been made to control structures to this level. Vocabulary is also strictly controlled where comprehension is necessary. However, low-frequency words can sometimes be found in the pronunciation exercises where practicing the production of specific sounds is the central goal.

Organization of the Text

Speak Up Book 2 is divided into two sections. Each section contains twelve units and two review units. The first half of the text covers consonant and vowel contrasts. The second half deals with stress, intonation, and linking.

An appendix at the back of the text provides mouth diagrams and a vowel chart.

Unit Organization

Each unit starts with a section called **Before you begin**. This is meant as a short warm-up activity to get students thinking about the topic.

Section A is a conversation that incorporates the target language presented within the unit. This section is totally receptive and students are not required to use any of the new language. Section B follows with sound discrimination and pronunciation exercises. Section C provides practice of the target sounds within more extended contexts. Section D is a combination of poems, chants, and conversations that aid in the development of rhythm in a more light-hearted way. The communicative exercises in Section E give students a chance to practice the new material in a less-structured manner. The last section of the unit is entitled **Looking Ahead to the TOEFL® Test**. Units 1–8 contain practice material for section A, units 9–21 provide practice for section B, and units 22-28 for section C of the listening comprehension section of the TOEFL® examination.

Using the Text

Before you begin. The purpose of this section is to promote student involvement in the situational context of the conversation. It can be done with the entire class, as groupwork or as pairwork. Students working on their own in the laboratory should be encouraged to read the questions and think about the answers. This section should take no more than five minutes of class time.

Section A. It is important that students read the listening comprehension questions before they actually listen to the conversation. This will aid their comprehension by providing them with a focus. If students seem dubious after listening to the conversation once, do not hesitate to play it for them again before you go over the answers to the questions.

Sections B–D. In these sections students may encounter unknown and obscure vocabulary words that have been included for practice of particular sounds. Students should be encouraged to repeat the words even though they may not understand them.
   Students may easily become frustrated trying to pronounce difficult sounds. Make sure they understand that being able to hear these difficult sounds is an important preliminary step to being able to pronounce them and that they should not feel discouraged if they cannot say them immediately.

Section E. Since this section contains freer activities, there are times that students will be able to avoid the target language if they want. Therefore, teachers should encourage their students to use the structures and sounds of the unit as much as possible. It may sometimes be helpful to precede the activity with a model that uses some of the target language.

Looking Ahead to the TOEFL® Test. This section provides practice for the listening comprehension section of the TOEFL® examination and may be used in class or assigned to students for independent self-study. Answers are provided on the Tapescript/Answer Key, available upon request.

Mouth Diagrams and Vowel Chart

Many students will be unfamiliar with the use of the mouth diagrams and vowel chart. It would be helpful to spend some time at the beginning of the course showing students how to interpret and use them. Note that the mouth diagrams are depicted in an appendix on page 101.

Audio Program

A multi-cassette audio program contains all of the listening material teachers will need to structure a dynamic aural/oral skills program. A sample cassette is available upon request.

unit 1

Nothing Ventured, Nothing Gained

In this unit you will practice: pronunciation of /ʌ/ / /ɑ/ (nut/not)

Pronunciation Tool
See page 102.

Before you begin: Discuss the following questions with your classmates.

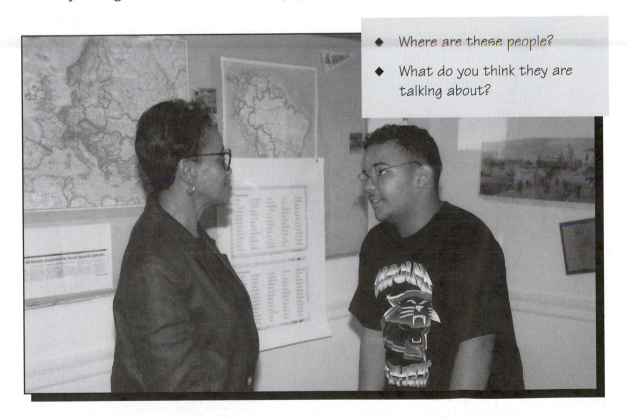

◆ Where are these people?

◆ What do you think they are talking about?

A. **Read the questions. Then listen to the conversation and answer them.**

1. Lionel's problem is with
   a. pronunciation.   **b.** reading.   **c.** spelling.

2. How many reasons does Lionel give for not looking up words in the dictionary?
   a. one   **b.** two   **c.** three

3. Lionel thinks the pronunciation symbols are
 a. interesting.   **b.** ridiculous.   **c.** funny.

4. The word the teacher asked Lionel to write is spelled
 a. prominent.   **b.** prominint.   **c.** prominant.

B. **Look at these two words and the symbol for the pronunciation of the vowel.**

nut /ʌ/   not /ɑ/

Listen and repeat these words.

1. under   **2.** stock   **3.** love   **4.** money   **5.** father   **6.** mother

7. public   **8.** luck   **9.** calm   **10.** fond   **11.** come   **12.** bomb

Now listen and repeat the words again. Put them in the column under *nut* or *not*.

nut /ʌ/	*not* /ɑ/
_____	_____
_____	_____
_____	_____
_____	_____
_____	_____
_____	_____
_____	_____

C. **Listen to these sentences and write the missing words.**

1. She gave him a big _____.

2. There's a big _____ in that corner.

3. The _____ is late today.

4. It's really _____ in the _____.

5. It's not a very big _____.

D. **Look back at the title of this unit and then answer the questions below.**

    1. Look up the two words *venture* and *gain* in your dictionary.

    2. Which of the following sentences is similar in meaning to the title?
        a. If you want to be successful, you have to take risks.
        b. There is nothing you can do to gain success.

    3. Listen to the conversation. Who says "Nothing ventured, nothing gained"?

    4. Listen to the conversation again and complete the chart below.

Time	Place	Location
2:00	Study Now Institute	_____
_____	_____	corner of Hemlock and Billings
4:00–6:00	_____	_____
_____	Fun for the Young Language School	_____

E. **Talking Together. With your partner, follow the instructions below.**

    1. Look up the following words in the dictionary. Look at the phonetic symbols. Try to pronounce the words correctly. Listen to the tape and check your pronunciation.

        job   appointment

        tuition   fun

        apply   luck

    2. Take turns.

        STUDENT A: Read your partner the definition of one of the words from the list.
        STUDENT B: Listen to the definition. Make up a sentence that uses the word
                       your partner has defined.

F. Looking Ahead to the TOEFL® TEST

Listen to each sentence. Then read the four choices. Circle the answer that is closest in meaning to the sentence you heard on the tape.

1. A) The public offices are near the stairs.

   B) The phones are not for public use.

   C) The phones under the stairs are for public use.

   D) The public fund is under revision.

2. A) The meeting was very calm.

   B) Please come to the meeting.

   C) There aren't usually a lot of people at these meetings.

   D) Note the people that came to the meeting.

3. A) Ruth doesn't have a job, but Sally does.

   B) Both Ruth and Sally work together.

   C) Sally has a job, but Ruth doesn't.

   D) Both Ruth and Sally are out of work.

4. A) I've never had bad luck in my life.

   B) My luck is worse now than at any other time in my life.

   C) All my life I've had bad luck.

   D) Life is always full of bad things.

unit 2

Dead Men Tell No Tales

In this unit you will practice: pronunciation of /ɪ/ /ɛ/ (*mit / met*)

> **Pronunciation Tool**
> **See page 102.**

Before you begin: Discuss the following question with your classmates.

◆ What kind of information can you get from a newspaper?

A. **Read the statements. Then listen to the conversation and complete them.**

1. Mitch is reading a
   a. magazine.   **b.** report.   **c.** newspaper.

2. Mr. Chen hit his head on the
   a. bin.   **b.** bed.   **c.** desk.

3. Mr. Chen was
   a. rich.   **b.** sick.   **c.** in debt.

4. Bill
   a. is ten now.   **b.** is six now.   **c.** was ten when he met Mr. Chen.

B. Listen and circle the words you hear.

1.	sit	set	6.	knit	net
2.	till	tell	7.	lit	let
3.	rid	red	8.	disk	desk
4.	miss	mess	9.	did	dead
5.	Sid	said	10.	lift	left

Listen again and repeat the words you hear.

Now listen and repeat these sentences.

1. Sit till I tell you what Sid said.
2. Lynn lifted the lid and let it go.

C. Listen to this message on a telephone answering machine. Then read it aloud.

This is Kim calling Mr. Smith. I need to talk to you. Mr. Chen is dead and there's a problem with his will. Tell Tim to get rid of the rest. Okay? Bye.

Now listen to this message. Fill the spaces with *i* or *e*.

K__m. Th__s __s Mr. Smith. I got your m__ssage, but there's

another probl__m. T__m can't get r__d of the r__st. Can you

g__t S__d to do ___t? And what's the probl__m with the w__ll?

G__ve me a call. Bye.

Now read the second message aloud.

D. Listen to the conversation and identify the people.

People: Wendy, Tim, Mick, Mr. Chen

_____ _____   _____ _____

Why do you think the title of this unit is "Dead men tell no tales"?

E. **Talking Together. Fill out the chart about yourself. Then interview a classmate and complete the chart.**

Example:

STUDENT A: I met my best friend at school when I was ten.
Where did you meet your best friend?

STUDENT B: I met my best friend at a party.

	Where	When
I met my best friend _____ met his or her best friend		
I read my last book _____ read his or her last book		
I last went to the movies _____ last went to the movies		
I took my last trip _____ took his or her last trip		
I last went to swim _____ last went to swim		

Listen to each sentence. Then read the four choices. Circle the answer that is closest in meaning to the sentence you heard on the tape.

1. **A)** She didn't spill the juice.

   B) She didn't spell the word.

   C) She can't spell at all.

   D) She didn't spill the water.

2. **A)** He relates to people very well.

   B) He gets a lot of presents from people.

   C) He got on the bus with a lot of people.

   D) He gets on the bus at 8 A.M.

3. **A)** Bill didn't do well on the exam although he studied hard.

   B) Bill did well on the exam even though he didn't study hard.

   C) Because he studied hard, Bill did well on his exam.

   D) Bill didn't study, so he didn't do well on his exam.

4. **A)** More people came to this concert than to the last one.

   B) Not many people came to the last concert.

   C) Fewer people came to the last concert than to this one.

   D) Fewer people came to this concert than to the last one.

unit 3

A Friend in Need Is a Friend Indeed

In this unit you will practice: pronunciation of /oʷ/ /ɔ/(low/law)

> **Pronunciation Tool**
> see page 102.

Before you begin: Discuss the following questions with your classmates.

◆ What do you think the man on the right is saying?

◆ How can you get a loan in your country?

A. **Read the sentences. Then listen to the conversation and answer TRUE or FALSE.**

1. Farouk's friend bought a car. _____

2. Joe needs more money. _____

3. Farouk has lots of money. _____

4. Farouk has to fill out a form. _____

B. Listen to these words:

saw	law	fall	lawn	daughter
jaw	tall	ball	lost	borrow

All these words include the vowel sound written phonetically as / ɔ /. Now listen again and repeat the words.

Listen to these words:

sew	low	boat	gold	know
row	bowl	coat	don't	cold

All these words include the vowel sound written phonetically as /oʷ/. Listen again and repeat the words.

Not all words that end in *ow* have the /oʷ/ sound. For example, look at this sentence and listen:

How now brown cow.

In these words the *ow* sound is written phonetically as /aʊ/. Listen to the sentence again and repeat it.

How now brown cow.

C. These words are the past-tense forms of some verbs. Read them aloud. Which sound do they have, /aʊ/ or / ɔ /?

bought	caught
brought	fought
taught	thought

Now listen to the tape and repeat the words.

Write the past tense of the correct verb from the list above.

1. He _____ a big ball for his daughter at the store.

2. She _____ the dog to give her its paw.

3. They _____ the exam was difficult.

4. They _____ five fish in the river.

5. The boys _____ over the new ball.

Now listen to the sentences and check your answers. Repeat the sentences.

D. **Listen to the conversation and put the pictures in order.**

Listen to the first conversation again. Answer the questions.

1. Who says "A friend in need is a friend indeed"?

2. Who is the friend indeed?

3. Are people who do not help their friends when they need help really friends?

E. **Talking Together. Write down:**

1. three things that you want.

2. three things that you've bought recently.

3. three things that you've borrowed.

Tell your partner. Ask if he or she had any of the same things on his or her list. Then tell your classmates what things you and your partner had in common.

Looking Ahead to the **TOEFL® TEST**

Listen to each sentence. Then read the four choices. Circle the answer that is closest in meaning to the sentence you heard on the tape.

1. **A)** These shoes usually cost 20 dollars.

   B) It's impossible to buy shoes like this for 20 dollars.

   C) This shows you what you can get in a good sale.

   D) There was a sale today, and I bought these shoes for 20 dollars.

2. **A)** The book wasn't interesting at all.

   B) I thought the book would be extremely interesting.

   C) I didn't think the book would be interesting, and I was right.

   D) I didn't think the book would be interesting, but actually it was.

3. **A)** Mr. Moat teaches in law school.

   B) Mr. Moat never taught in law school.

   C) Mr. Moat likes to teach in law school.

   D) Mr. Moat taught in law school before.

4. **A)** The coat was made of gold.

   B) The director played with the gold.

   C) The director put a border of gold onto the coat.

   D) The gold braid was never put on the coat.

Practice Makes Perfect

In this unit you will practice: pronunciation of /fl/ /fr/ *(fly/fry)* and /pl/ /pr/ *(play/pray)*

Pronunciation Tool
See page 101.

Before you begin: Discuss the following questions with your classmates.

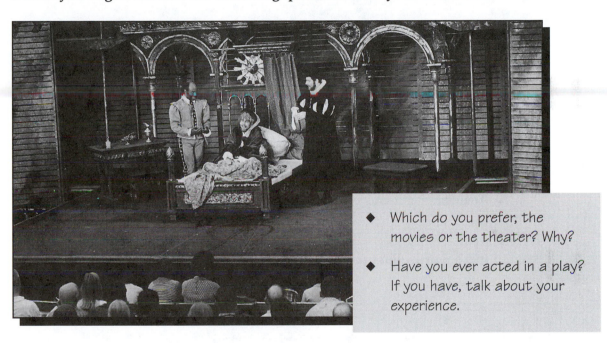

- ◆ Which do you prefer, the movies or the theater? Why?

- ◆ Have you ever acted in a play? If you have, talk about your experience.

A. Read the questions. Then listen to the conversation and answer them.

1. Fred has to practice
   a. a little.   **b.** some.   **c.** a lot.

2. Who says "Practice makes perfect"?
   a. Fred   **b.** Paul   **c.** no one

3. The two people are talking about
   a. a hijacking.   **b.** a play.   **c.** a plane.

4. The flight begins in
   a. Paris.   **b.** Plymouth.   **c.** Broadway.

5. The plane is
   a. dramatic.   **b.** hijacked.   **c.** ready.

B. Listen and circle the words you hear.

1. fly   fry
2. flea   free
3. flute   fruit
4. flight   fright
5. flame   frame

Listen again and repeat the words.

Listen and write the sentences you hear.

1. A _____ can't _____.
2. The _____ on the flight is _____.
3. There was a _____ on the _____.
4. The _____ fell on the _____.

Listen and write *pr* or *pl*.

1. That's a _____etty nice _____ace.
2. _____ease _____omise to _____ay something.
3. There are _____enty of other things to _____actice.
4. The _____ince's _____oject is _____ivate.

C. Listen to these words. For each one, put a check in the correct column.

	fl	fr	pl	pr
1.				
2.				
3.				
4.				
5.				
6.				
7.				
8.				
9.				
10.				

Now repeat the words.

D. Listen to the conversation. Under the correct date, write the name of the person who does the activity.

	Friday 9th	Saturday 10th	Thursday 15th	Friday 16th	Saturday 17th
1. play cards					
2. play the flute					
3. go to the airport					
4. probably pick up the programs					
5. present the play					

E. Talking Together. With three or four of your classmates, write a short conversation. The following topics may give you some ideas.

Going to the doctor or dentist

Planning a trip or a party

Arriving too late at the airport to catch a plane

Teaching English to students

F. Looking Ahead to the TOEFL® TEST

Listen to each sentence. Then read the four choices. Circle the answer that is closest in meaning to the sentence you heard on the tape.

1. **A)** Please come by yourself, Frieda.

   B) Worry about yourself, Frieda.

   C) Frieda, you should act naturally.

   D) Don't worry if you come by yourself, Frieda.

2. **A)** Fred never seems to get frustrated.

   B) Fred gets frustrated, but I've never seen him.

   C) Fred gets frustrated easily.

   D) Fred's gotten frustrated only once.

3. **A)** Please put the report on the desk.

   B) I've reported the problem with the printer.

   C) Put some paper into the printer.

   D) I'd like you to print out this report.

4. **A)** Fritz fixed the frame last week.

   B) Fritz didn't fix the frame last week.

   C) Fritz is going to fix the frame next week.

   D) Fritz shouldn't fix the frame next week.

unit 5

Don't Count Your Chickens Before They're Hatched

In this unit you will practice: pronunciation
of /br/ /bl/ *(brink/blink)* and /dr/ /tr/ *(dry/try)*

Pronunciation Tool
See page 101.

Before you begin: Discuss the following questions with your classmates.

◆ People who count their chickens before they're hatched sometimes are disappointed. Can you explain why?

◆ One of these men is going on a fishing vacation. How do you think it will turn out?

A. Read the sentences. Then listen to the conversation and complete them.

1. Check the things that need to be fixed on Drew's car.
   a) brakes   d) trunk
   b) wheels   e) tires
   c) lights

2. Drew plans to catch
   a) salmon.   b) trout.   c) sharks.

3. Drew is going to fish in a
   a) lake.   b) sea.   c) river.

4. If it rains, Drew is going to stay in
   a) his car.   b) his cabin.   c) his tent.

B. **Listen and repeat the following pairs of words.**

brink	blink
brand	bland
breed	bleed
brew	blue
broom	bloom

Listen and fill in the spaces with *br* or *bl*.

1. I _____ ought the _____ ue _____ oom.

2. The _____ ond girl ate _____ an for _____ unch.

3. He _____ inked when he realized how _____ and that _____ and tasted.

Now say each sentence aloud.

C. **Listen and repeat the following pairs of words.**

dry	try
drew	true
drip	trip
drunk	trunk
drench	trench
drought	trout

Listen and fill in the spaces with *dr* or *tr*.

1. I _____ ew a _____ ue picture of the _____ ain.

2. The _____ unk was _____ enched in the _____ ench.

3. I'll _____ y to _____ y it.

Now say each sentence aloud.

D.   Listen to the conversation and put the pictures in order.

E.   Talking Together. With your partner, make up a conversation between Blake and Drew in Brighton. The following clues may help you.

How . . . ?

Tell me what . . . ?

What . . . doctor . . . ?

Can you . . . ?

How many fish . . . ?

Read your conversation to the class.

F. Looking Ahead to the TOEFL® TEST

Listen to each sentence. Then read the four choices. Circle the answer that is closest in meaning to the sentence you heard on the tape.

1. **A)** I'll call you unless Trish brings the blanket.

    B) I won't call you if Trish brings the blanket.

    C) Trish may bring the blanket, and then I'll call you.

    D) I'll call you even though Trish doesn't bring the blanket.

2. **A)** Bruce fixed the brakes.

    B) The boy next door didn't fix the brakes.

    C) The boy next door fixed the brakes.

    D) The boy next door asked Bruce to fix the brakes.

3. **A)** Trevor doesn't want to take a trip to Bremen.

    B) Both Brad and Trevor want to take a trip to Bremen.

    C) Brad doesn't want Trevor to take a trip to Bremen.

    D) Neither Brad nor Trevor wants to take a trip to Bremen.

4. **A)** Eighty trees were brought.

    B) We brought twenty trees.

    C) Forty trees are all we need.

    D) We really need eighty trees.

unit 6

Good Riddance to Bad Rubbish

In this unit you will practice: pronunciation of /kl/ /kr/ (*clown/crown*) and /gl/ /gr/ (*glow/grow*)

Pronunciation Tool
See page 101.

Before you begin: Discuss the following question with your classmates.

◆ What do you think this woman is reading about?

A. Read the questions. Then listen to the conversation and answer them.

1. What is Claudia reading?

2. Who is Graham?

3. Why does Greg say "Good riddance to bad rubbish"?

4. Who made the supper?

5. What did he make?

6. Who forgot the crackers?

B. **Look at these pairs of words. Listen and underline the words you hear.**

clown	crown	gloom	groom
clamp	cramp	gland	grand
clash	crash	glow	grow
clam	cram	glean	green
clank	crank	glade	grade
cloak	croak	glass	grass

Say the words you underlined. Then repeat each pair of words.

C. **Work with your partner.**

STUDENT A: Choose a word from each column above and try to say the words one after the other quickly.

EXAMPLE: **clam, crash, gland, grade**

STUDENT B: Listen and draw lines to connect the words your partner read. Then read your partner's words back to him or her.

D. **Read the following poem silently while listening to the tape. Then follow the instructions below.**

Oh no!
Says the clown all dressed in brown.
My long green nose—see how it grows.
Soon it will clash
With my bright red sash.
It will make a fine crutch
Though I don't know how much
I can use it for walking
'Cause I really need it for talking.

1. Underline the words that begin with *cl*, *cr*, *gl*, or *gr*.

2. Say the words.

3. Now recite the poem to your partner or to your class.

E.   **Talking Together. Look at the pictures and follow the instructions below.**

1. Use the pictures to write a continuation of the story Claudia is reading.

2. Listen to your partner's story.

3. Number the pictures from 1 to 6 according to the order your partner uses.

4. Tell your partner's version of the story to the class.

F. Looking Ahead to the TOEFL® TEST

Listen to each sentence. Then read the four choices. Circle the answer that is closest in meaning to the sentence you heard on the tape.

1. **A)** Possibly Claire went downtown to buy some glasses.

    B) Claire had to go downtown to buy some glasses.

    C) Claire wasn't planning on going downtown to buy some glasses.

    D) For sure, Claire went downtown to buy some glasses.

2. **A)** Did you see that cloud?

    B) It's really cloudy today.

    C) I feel great on cloudy days.

    D) It was cloudy yesterday.

3. **A)** Your grandfather didn't have any problems.

    B) Your grandfather didn't close the account.

    C) Your grandfather had problems because he closed the account.

    D) Your grandfather had problems because he didn't close the account.

4. **A)** The last date to pay your credit card is March 10.

    B) You must pay your credit card after March 10.

    C) You can pay your credit card only on March 10.

    D) They have to give you your credit card on March 10.

unit 7

Review

A. Read the questions. Then listen to the conversation and answer them.

1. The man is in a
   a. bookstore. **b.** library. **c.** drugstore.

2. Which of the following can be checked out?
   a. *New Age Encyclopedia* **b.** *Time* magazine **c.** a novel

3. Which of the following services are not mentioned as being available?
   a. CD-ROM **b.** documentary movies **c.** photocopies

4. Which of the following kinds of identification does the man have?
   a. student ID **b.** credit card **c.** driver's license

B. Listen again to the conversation. Can you hear any words that begin with *fl, pl, bl, cl,* or *gl?* Write them in the correct column.

fl	pl	bl	cl	gl
_____	_____	_____	_____	_____
			_____	
			_____	

Listen again to the conversation. Can you hear any words that begin with *fr, pr, br, dr, tr, cr,* or *gr?* Write them in the correct column.

fr	pr	br	dr	tr	cr	gr
_____	_____	_____	_____	_____	_____	_____
_____			_____			

C. **Listen to these sentences and fill in the missing words.**

1. I can _____ some _____, _____ you like.

2. He does _____ want to go to _____ school.

3. They _____ that new movie, _____ they didn't like
   _____ .

4. We've _____ a _____ of our neighbors.

5. _____ me see—I _____ you _____ a computer.

D. **Here are some of the words that you have seen in Units 1 – 6. Use the words to write questions and sentences.**

EXAMPLE: Paul has a new job.
Did you look under the desk?

luck	money	father	mother	public	sit	miss	left	tell
fix	bought	taught	brought	thought	loan	tall	ball	fry
free	flight	play	profit	print	blue	trip	dry	blond
clown	green	grow	job	under	desk	great	true	bright

Now dictate your sentences and questions to your partner.

Check with your partner to see if you wrote them correctly.

E. **Ask your partner about his or her reading habits. The following phrases may help.**

How often / library   What / last book

How many books / read   What / best book

What kind of books / like   Important / studies

Prefer / books / movies   Read / before / sleep

F. Looking Ahead to the TOEFL® TEST

Listen to each sentence. Then read the four choices. Circle the answer that is closest in meaning to the sentence you heard on the tape.

1. A) Naturally, Mrs. Miller is a good printer.

   B) Mrs. Miller is a member of a printers' association.

   C) Mrs. Miller has belonged for a long time.

   D) The national printer belongs to Mrs. Miller.

2. A) Underprivileged children will sell certain products.

   B) Sales of some products will bring large profits.

   C) Underprivileged children will make some products to sell.

   D) Underprivileged children will receive the profits from sales of some products.

3. A) That new broom was just bought for the house.

   B) The broom for the house wasn't new.

   C) I really need to buy a new broom for the house.

   D) No one has bought a new broom for a long time.

4. A) The children didn't want to play with the clown.

   B) The children and the clown played on the grass.

   C) The children and the clown played with the grass.

   D) The children didn't play on the grass with the clown.

Where There's Smoke, There's Fire

In this unit you will practice: pronunciation of
/sk/ /skw/ /sp/ /sl/ /sm/ /st/ (*sky/squeeze/spell/slip/small/still*)

Pronunciation Tool
See page 101.

Before you begin: Discuss the following questions with your classmates.

◆ What is happening in this picture?

◆ Would you like to be on this boat? Why or why not?

A. **Listen to the news bulletin. Then answer TRUE or FALSE.**

1. The schooner was from Scotland. _____

2. The storm arose the night of the sixteenth. _____

3. Captain Smith smelled the smoke. _____

4. The storm didn't affect the equipment on the schooner. _____

B.   Work with your partner.

STUDENT A: Choose a word from each column. Try to say the words one after the other quickly.

EXAMPLE: **sky, squash, speech, sled, smell, stop**

STUDENT B: Listen and draw lines to connect the words your partner read. Then read your partner's words back to him or her.

sky	squirrel	spill	slip	smile	still
skate	squeeze	spell	slam	smell	stop
skill	squalid	spend	sled	smoke	storm
scratch	squirt	speech	slight	smog	start
school	squash	spurt	slap	smart	step

C.   Read the following poem silently while listening to the tape.

Have you ever skipped in time,
Have you ever read a rhyme,
Have you ever smiled a smile,
Just to say "Be friends awhile"?

Have you ever smelled a fresh-picked rose,
Or stared out windows when it snows?
Have you ever squeezed a friend,
And told him "Love will never end"?

Underline the words that begin with *st*, *sm*, or *squ*. Say the words.

Now recite the poem.

D. **Listen to the reporter's interview with Captain Slade Smith. Fill in the blanks with the correct words.**

REPORTER: How do you feel today, Captain Smith?

CAPTAIN: Fine, much better. The _____ people here have been very kind. I'd like to come back and _____ a few days' vacation here.

REPORTER: Hopefully, you'll be able to do that, sir. Tell me, Captain, do you know what _____ the fire?

CAPTAIN: No, no, I don't. There's a _____ committee investigating that right now. But a fire like that was certainly very _____.

REPORTER: I think you said you were _____ at the time the fire _____?

CAPTAIN: Yes, I was. The _____ of the _____ woke me up. I rang the alarm, and everyone helped to put out the fire, but it had already done a lot of damage.

E. **Talking Together. Continue the interview.**

STUDENT A: You are the reporter.

STUDENT B: You are Captain Smith.

The following words may help you.

What time . . . ?

Then what . . . ?

How many . . . hurt?

What . . . destroy?

How long . . . ?

Read your interview to the class.

F. Looking Ahead to the TOEFL® TEST

Listen to each sentence. Then read the four choices. Circle the answer that is closest in meaning to the sentence you heard on the tape.

1. **A)** After Juan slept, his toothache got better.

   B) Juan's toothache made him sleep a long time.

   C) Juan got a toothache after he slept so long.

   D) Juan had a toothache, and he didn't sleep.

2. **A)** The storm last January was really bad.

   B) The storm last January really scared them.

   C) There were bad storms all through January.

   D) I was scared during the storm in January.

3. **A)** Was the movie strange?

   B) The movie was strange.

   C) The movie was sad.

   D) Did you see that strange movie?

4. **A)** I also go to that school.

   B) Two people went to that school.

   C) They went to that school, too.

   D) I go to two schools.

unit *9*

Better Late Than Never

In this unit you will practice: pronunciaton of /str/ /skr/ /spr/
(*strike/scratch/sprint*)

> **Pronunciation Tool**
> **See page 101.**

Before you begin: Discuss the following questions with your classmates.

◆ Where are these people?

◆ What kinds of announcements might they hear?

A. **Read the sentences. Then listen to the announcements and complete them.**

1. The little girl is
   a) nine years old.
   b) five years old.
   c) two years old.

2. The passenger service desk is near
   a) gate 2.
   b) gate 12.
   c) gate 10.

3. There will be a delay of approximately three hours due to
   a) exceptionally cold weather.
   b) exceptionally strong winds.
   c) exceptionally heavy rain.

4. a) Dinner
   b) Brunch   will be served in the Spruce Room.
   c) Lunch

B. Listen to the announcements again and circle the words you hear.

1. stroke   2. stroll   3. Sprock   4. scrape

5. straight   6. scratch   7. striped   8. strike

9. Strasbourg   10. strong   11. sprint   12. Spruce

Listen and repeat the words you circled.

Work with a partner.

STUDENT A: Dictate five words from the list to your partner.
STUDENT B: Write down the words your partner dictates. Check with your partner to make sure you spelled the words correctly.

Read, listen, and repeat this sentence.

The man in the straight, striped jacket sitting in the Spruce Room is Mr. Sprock from Strasbourg.

Make up other sentences with the words above. Then read the sentences to your partner.

C. Silently read this conversation between Mr. Sprock and the person on the white courtesy telephone.

MR. SPROCK: Hello.
PERSON: Hello, Mr. Jim Sprock?
MR. SPROCK: Yes, who is this, please?
PERSON: Never mind. That's not important. But you have something I want.
MR. SPROCK: That's strange. I only have my own suitcase.
PERSON: It's not strange at all. There are some extra screws at the bottom of your suitcase. Undo the screws and you will see a package with a scrap of paper on it. Take the suitcase to the address written on the scrap of paper.
MR. SPROCK: And if I don't?
PERSON: Then, your wife will have a little problem. If you take the suitcase to that address on Klondike Street, she will be there waiting for you.
MR. SPROCK: OK, I'm going, but if you hurt my wife, I will strike out at you with all the strength I have.
PERSON: See you soon, Mr. Sprock.

Take turns reading the conversation aloud. Then discuss the following questions with your partner.

1. What do you think is in Mr. Sprock's suitcase?

2. Who do you think is the person on the phone?

3. What do you think will happen to Mr. Sprock and his wife?

D. Listen to the conversation and do the activities.

1. Who said it? Write *Silvia* or *Mrs. Strumford*.

    a) I wasn't paying attention. _____

    b) The flight to Strasbourg has been delayed three hours. _____

    c) Better late than never. _____

    d) That's easy for you to say. _____

2. With your partner, make up a conversation between Silvia and Rob when Silvia finally arrives in Strasbourg.

3. Read your conversation to the class.

E. Talking Together. Think of three places you'd like to visit. List them in the chart below. Then invent flight numbers and departure times.

Destination	Flight	Departure Time

Ask your partner where she or he would like to go, the flight number, and the departure time, and add this information to your chart.

Listen to each sentence. Then read the four choices. Circle the answer that is closest in meaning to the sentence you heard on the tape.

1.   **A)** She's wearing my striped sweater.

    B) I don't know where my striped sweater is.

    C) Wear my striped sweater, if you like.

    D) Where did you see my sweater?

2.   **A)** The bank is straight ahead.

    B) Do that before you go to the bank.

    C) Please straighten the bag.

    D) Go directly to the bank.

3.   **A)** I went to fix the screen.

    B) I want to work with a screen.

    C) I went to get the screen.

    D) I would like to buy a screen.

4.   **A)** Barbara likes her work because she doesn't have any stress.

    B) Barbara has a lot of stress, but she likes her job anyway.

    C) Barbara thinks it's good to have some stress at work.

    D) Barbara doesn't like her work because of the stress.

Make Hay While the Sun Shines

In this unit you will practice: pronunciation of /θ/ /t/ /s/
(*thank/tank/sank*)

Pronunciation Tool
See page 101.

Before you begin: Discuss the following questions with your classmates.

◆ Who is this woman?

◆ Where do you think she is?

A. Read the questions. Then listen to the conversation and answer them.

1. How many awards did Whitney Houston receive?

2. For what kind of song did she receive the awards?

3. What does Theo want to buy?

4. Why can't Sam go with him?

5. Who says "I'd better make hay while the sun shines"?

6. "Make hay while the sun shines" means
   a) work while you have daylight.
   b) work while everything is in your favor.
   c) work in the field while there is sun.

B. **Look at the list of words below. Listen and circle the ones you hear.**

thin	tin	sin
thank	tank	sank
theme	team	seem
thick	tick	sick
thought	taught	sought
thigh	tie	sigh
thongs	tongs	songs

Listen again and repeat the words.

Now repeat all the words again. Notice where you put your tongue for each of the sounds.

C. **Listen to these sentences and fill in the missing words.**

1. The _____ man _____ he _____ a ghost.

2. He _____ her how to _____ her shoes.

3. He _____ into the _____ mud.

4. The _____ is near the _____.

5. The _____ _____ was _____.

Now repeat the sentences.

D. **Read this chant. Fill in the blanks with words from the list.**

thought   head   thief   friend
team   sale   tree

Sing a song

All day long

Tell a tale

Make a _____

Catch a _____

Trust a chief

Tie a thread

Lift your _____

Plant a _____

Bend your knee

Teach your _____

Mend each seam

Think a _____

Work a lot

Thank a _____

Here's the end.

Now listen to the chant. Check your answers.

Now say the chant.

E. **Talking Together. Make a list of songs and singers that you like. Ask your partner what songs and singers he or she chose. With your partner, decide which songs and singers you would like to give an award to.**

F. Looking Ahead to the TOEFL® TEST

Listen to each sentence. Then read the four choices. Circle the answer that is closest in meaning to the sentence you heard on the tape.

1. **A)** We just finished studying the new topics when we heard the songs.

    B) We were going to study the new topics when we heard the songs.

    C) At the time we were studying the new topics, someone nearby sang some songs.

    D) Some new students were studying the topics.

2. **A)** It seems that people are less thoughtful now than before.

    B) It seems that people used to see sad things there.

    C) It seems that people are much more thoughtful now than before.

    D) They are going to get some new things for the team.

3. **A)** Sam's glad he asked about the texts.

    B) Which texts did Sam ask about?

    C) The texts were about different themes.

    D) Sam's sorry he didn't ask about the texts.

4. **A)** Terry received Timothy's card last night.

    B) Terry's letter came last night.

    C) Timothy phoned Terry at 11:30 P.M. last night.

    D) Timothy's going to send Terry a card later.

Money Doesn't Grow on Trees

In this unit you will practice: pronunciation of final /st/ /sk/ /rt/ /ft/ (*fast/desk/skirt/lift*)

Before you begin: Discuss the following questions with your classmates.

Flowers?

◆ Look at the title. What does it mean?

◆ What do you think these people are talking about?

A. **Read the questions. Then listen to the conversation and answer them.**

1. Who does Bart want to buy a gift for?

2. What is Bart's problem?

3. What suggestions does Curt make?

4. Which of Curt's suggestions does Bart like?

B. Listen to the conversation again. Circle the words you hear.

  1. fast   2. gift   3. lift   4. last   5. ask

  6. desk   7. must   8. risk   9. heart   10. almost

  11. mask   12. left   13. skirt   14. ghost   15. disc

Listen and repeat the words you circled.

C. Bart wanted to give his girlfriend the compact disc with a special card. He found a poem, called a limerick, that he thought he might be able to use. Read and listen to the limerick.

> There was a young maid who said "Why
> Can't I look in my ear with my eye?
> If I give my mind to it,
> I'm sure I can do it,
> You never can tell till you try."
>
> *Edward Lear*

Read the limerick aloud.

Bart thought he could write his own limerick. Listen and fill in the missing words.

There was a young _____ with a _____

Full of _____ and desire to impart,

Who said, "Here is my _____

Please take it and _____

My soul to a land full of _____ ."

D. Read the question. Then listen to the conversation and answer it.

What is Bart's problem now?

Work with your partner and write a limerick for Bart.

E. Talking Together. Read your limerick aloud to your classmates. Vote on the ones you like best. Ask the authors of those limericks to dictate them so you can make a collection of limericks.

F. Looking Ahead to the TOEFL® TEST

Listen to each sentence. Then read the four choices. Circle the answer that is closest in meaning to the sentence you heard on the tape.

1. **A)** Mr. Linsk went to the heart specialist a long time ago.

   B) Mr. Linsk didn't go to the heart specialist, although it would have been a good idea.

   C) Mr. Linsk didn't need to go to the heart specialist before.

   D) Mr. Linsk wanted to see the heart specialist, but he couldn't.

2. **A)** More than half the participants could test the product.

   B) Less than fifty participants couldn't test the product.

   C) About sixty percent of the participants couldn't test the product.

   D) About forty percent of the participants could test the product.

3. **A)** The last report on my desk is finished.

   B) The report on my desk is completely wrong.

   C) The last report on my desk is not finished.

   D) I'll report this last.

4. **A)** I went to the coast a long time ago.

   B) I've lived at the coast until now.

   C) I still haven't gone to the coast.

   D) This is the first time I've been to the coast.

unit **12**

If You Can't Beat 'Em, Join 'Em

In this unit you will practice: pronunciation of final /ŋ/ /ŋk/ (*sing/sink*)

Before you begin: Discuss the following questions with your classmates.

◆ Where are these people? What is their relationship?

◆ What questions might someone ask you at a job interview?

A. **Read the questions. Then listen to the job interview and answer them.**

1. What kind of job does Hank want?

2. He mentions three things that he thinks qualify him for the job. What are they?

3. Does Mrs. Wang think these things are important?

4. Who does Hank refer to when he says "If you can't beat 'em, join 'em"?

5. What else does Hank have to do besides the job interview?

6. When will Hank know whether he has been accepted?

B. Look at each pair of words. Circle the word you hear.

sing	sink	king	kink
bring	brink	thing	think
sang	sank	cling	clink
bang	bank	ping	pink
rang	rank		

Listen again and repeat the words.

Now listen again and repeat the pairs of words.

C. Write a sentence using some of the words from Exercise B.

EXAMPLE: Please bring me a pink sink.

Now dictate your sentence to your partner.

D. Listen to the chant and fill in the missing words.

Sing a _____ and _____ along.

Make a _____, but not a clang.

Sound the gong, you're not so _____.

You're on the brink? Have a _____.

_____ in _____, enjoy a wink.

Be a _____, not a thing.

Say the chant aloud.

E. Talking Together. With your partner, make up a job interview. Here are some suggestions for jobs you might apply for:

receptionist	teacher	truck driver
computer programmer	school counselor	security guard

F. Looking Ahead to the TOEFL® TEST

Listen to the conversation. Then someone will ask you a question. Read the four choices and circle the one that best answers the question.

1. A) Reading a book

    B) Listening to music

    C) Working on a report

    D) Watching a movie

2. A) That he should get there quickly

    B) That he should worry about not getting the material

    C) That they don't learn a lot in that class

    D) That he won't get there on time

3. A) That the noise really bothers him

    B) That the people are crazy

    C) That he can't hear any noise

    D) That the noise just went up

4. A) There's no problem about the man reading the newspaper.

    B) She doesn't want the man to read the newspaper.

    C) She doesn't want him to take all of the newspaper.

    D) He can read the newspaper later.

Actions Speak Louder Than Words

In this unit you will practice: pronunciation of syllabic l/n *(table/cotton)*

Before you begin: Discuss the following questions with your classmates.

◆ The man in the picture is holding a tax return. What is a tax return?

◆ Have you ever filled out a tax return?

A. **Read the questions. Then listen to the message and answer them.**

1. Who says "You have just reached the home of Hendl Ibsen"?

2. What do you think Martin's profession is?

3. From the message, which of the following words would you use to describe Hendl? Why?

   organized   poor   responsible   lazy

   disorganized   rich   irresponsible   hard-working

4. Do you like to leave messages on answering machines? Why or why not? Do you have an answering machine?

B. **Listen and repeat the following words.**

table	saddle
ladle	rattle
kettle	settle
cuddle	battle
puddle	eagle
riddle	brittle

Repeat the following sentences.

1. Put the kettle and the ladle on the table.

2. The saddle fell into the puddle.

3. Where the eagle went is a riddle.

Make up your own sentence, using some of the words from the list. Dictate your sentence to your partner.

C. **Listen and repeat the following words.**

written	cotton
kitten	listen
beaten	dozen
mitten	oven
bitten	sudden

Repeat the following sentences.

1. I've written her a dozen letters already.

2. The kitten has a white mitten.

3. The price of cotton can't be beaten.

Make up your own sentence, using some of the words from the list. Dictate your sentence to your partner.

D. **Read the questions. Then listen to the message and answer them.**

1. Go back to Exercise A, question 3. Would you still use the same words to describe Hendl? If not, how would you describe him?

2. Based on his message and his voice, draw a picture of Hendl. Compare your picture with that of your partner.

3. Hendl tells Martin "Actions speak louder than words" because

   a) Hendl wants Martin to speak loudly.

   b) Hendl wants Martin to use the right words.

   c) Martin accuses Hendl of *talking* about doing his work instead of *doing* his work.

E. **Talking Together. Read and listen to this chant.**

Victory is to battle as answer is to riddle.
Saddle is to horse as bow is to fiddle.
Pot is to ladle as boat is to paddle.
Small is to little as half is to middle.
Fasten is to belt as straighten is to tie.
Written is to write as bitten is to bite.

These kinds of sentences are called analogies. Work with your partner to make up other analogies. Read your analogies to the class.

F. Looking Ahead to the TOEFL® TEST

Listen to the conversation. Then someone will ask you a question. Read the four choices and circle the one that best answers the question.

1. **A)** She's written two invitations.

   B) She hasn't written any invitations.

   C) She's written a dozen invitations.

   D) She hasn't even written two invitations.

2. **A)** On a ship

   B) In a business office

   C) In a law firm

   D) At home

3. **A)** Lawyer

   B) Taxi driver

   C) Scientist

   D) Librarian

4. **A)** Tom fixed the oven.

   B) Tom didn't fix the oven.

   C) Tom always fixes things.

   D) Tom didn't see the oven.

unit 14

Review

A. **Read the questions. Then listen to the conversation and answer them.**

1. What time of year is it?

2. Are Tom and Stephanie workers or students?

3. Does Tom think that squid is a good thing to eat?

4. What is the problem with the roast beef?

5. Do you think Tom and Stephanie are going to enjoy their dinner after all?

B. **The following words were used in the conversation you just heard. They have the sounds you studied in Units 8 – 13. First, say them to yourself. Then listen to the tape and repeat them.**

think	special	Stephanie	first
spring	Tom	desk	thinking
muddle	studying	struggling	sudden
tired	so	squid	scrumptious
small	salad	scoops	strawberry
dressing	Roquefort	stick	something
roast	left	things	almost
calling			

Now listen to the conversation again. Put an _S_ beside the word if Stephanie says it, a _T_ if Tom says it, and a _W_ if the waiter says it. Sometimes the same word is said by more than one person.

C. Listening Bingo. This bingo board contains words from the units you have studied. Cross out each word you hear. When you complete a vertical line or a horizontal line, you have bingo.

B	I	N	G	O
skate	straight	thing	heart	almost
bring	riddle	smoke	eagle	storm
squeeze	scratch	songs	thank	lift
written	slight	speech	sprint	taught
start	kitten	smog	skirt	think

D. Listen to another limerick by Edward Lear. Then say the limerick to your partner.

There was a young lady of Wilts
Who walked up to Scotland on stilts;
When they said it was shocking
To show so much stocking,
She answered, "Then what about kilts?"

Try to complete this limerick.

There once was a squire in spring

Who thought he would try a new _____.

He went to the _____

And got a new rank

And now he thinks he's a _____.

Listen to the limerick on the tape and check your answers. Then say the limerick to your partner.

E. Talking Together. With two partners, write a conversation about going to a restaurant or ordering in a restaurant similar to the conversation in Exercise A. Act out your conversation in front of the class.

F. Looking Ahead to the TOEFL® TEST

Listen to the conversation. Then someone will ask you a question. Read the four choices and circle the one that best answers the question.

1. A) That the man should study for a few more minutes

   B) That he's going to get a good grade

   C) That he shouldn't put off studying until the last minute

   D) Cramming is a good way of studying

2. A) That she drinks a lot of coffee

   B) That she doesn't drink enough coffee

   C) That she should stop sleeping so much

   D) That she should sleep more than she usually does

3. A) That he doesn't want to work

   B) That he has a problem because he doesn't have any work

   C) That he wants to work with theoretical problems

   D) That things are not going well for him at work

4. A) Playing the guitar

   B) Playing the piano

   C) Dancing

   D) Playing tennis

Easier Said Than Done

In this unit you will practice: syllables and word stress

Before you begin: Discuss the following questions with your classmates.

◆ This customer has a problem. What might it be?

◆ Have you ever made a reservation? For what?

A. Read the questions. Then listen to the conversation and answer them.

1. Where does this conversation take place?

2. What is the problem?

3. How does the clerk offer to help?

4. What mistake did Mr. Johnson make?

5. Think of some other situations where you might tell someone "Easier said than done."

B. **Divide these words into syllables.**

EXAMPLE: re/ cord

Hilton	yesterday	mistake	called
convention	stayed	ridiculous	computer
hotel	called	reservation	terribly
away	needed	Sheraton	happy
across	embarrassed	unfortunately	incomprehensible

Stress is extremely important in English pronunciation. Stressed syllables are longer and louder than unstressed syllables. Look at the list of words. Listen to the conversation again. Write each word in the correct column.

1st syllable stress	2nd syllable stress	3rd syllable stress	4th syllable stress
	mistake		

Look at the dictionary and check your work.

C. Fluency Practice. Listen to these phrases and repeat them.

1. have a reservation
2. this is ridiculous
3. I'm so embarrassed
4. that's incomprehensible
5. I'm terribly sorry
6. I've always stayed
7. called yesterday
8. across the street
9. there's a convention

With a partner, recreate the conversation. It doesn't have to be exactly the same as the one in Exercise A.

D. Listen to the chant. Then repeat each line.

Change of Plans

I'd called the station and made a reservation,
I'd packed my bags and prepared to go,
I'd had absolutely no hesitation,
Until you said you needed me so.

E. Talking Together. Follow the instructions below.

STUDENT A: You arrive at an expensive restaurant with a group of friends. They have no record of your reservation, and they say that there are no free tables for this evening. Try to get a table.

STUDENT B: You work at an expensive restaurant. Student A comes in with a group of friends. Unfortunately, you have no record of his or her reservation. Politely tell the people that you cannot give them a table.

Listen to the conversation. Then someone will ask you a question. Read the four choices and circle the one that best answers the question.

1. **A)** He thinks it's a good idea to close the window.

   B) He thinks it's cold.

   C) He doesn't want to close the window.

   D) He wants to open the window.

2. **A)** Make a phone call

   B) Go to the bank

   C) Write a postcard

   D) Make a list

3. **A)** Lawyer and client

   B) Doctor and nurse

   C) Father and daughter

   D) Teacher and student

4. **A)** A blue suit

   B) A black suit

   C) A black shirt

   D) A practical shirt

unit *16*

Business Before Pleasure

In this unit you will practice: reduced syllables

Before you begin: Discuss the following questions with your classmates.

- ◆ In the U.S., people often say "Business before pleasure." What do you think they mean?

- ◆ Where do you think these two people are working?

A. Read the questions. Then listen to the conversation and answer them.

1. Do Darlene and Frank see each other often?

2. Do they work for the same company? Did they ever?

3. What does Frank's company want Darlene to do?

B. **Sometimes an unstressed syllable disappears or changes its sound in normal speech. Listen to the words** *average* **and** *temperature* **in these examples:**

average, temperature   What's the average temperature?

What changes do you hear when the words are in a sentence?

Listen to these words and divide them into syllables. Then listen again and circle the sounds that disappear or change.

average	business	certainly	chocolate
comfortable	corporate	covering	difference
elementary	environment	everything	family
favorite	federal	frightening	history
interesting	laboratory	listener	mathematics
miserable	separate	several	vegetable

Listen and repeat the words.

C. **Fluency Practice. Listen and repeat the sentences. Build them up from right to left.**

1. Vegetables and chocolate are his favorite foods.

2. Businesspeople like the corporate environment.

3. His family is full of interesting mathematicians.

4. The average temperature in February is very low.

5. There are federal regulations for manufacturers.

D. **Listen to the chant. Then repeat it line by line.**

A Self-Satisfied Student

History, mathematics, it's all the same to me,
Everything's so easy, well certainly for me,
I've got an A average so I'm comfortable you see,
History, mathematics, it's all the same to me.

E. **Talking Together. With a partner, make up a conversation with as many of the words from the list in Exercise B as you can. Then perform the conversation for your class.**

Listen to the conversation. Then someone will ask you a question. Read the four choices and circle the one that best answers the question.

1. **A)** The father likes his son.

   B) He's a very quiet politician.

   C) Only the son is a politician.

   D) Both father and son are good politicians.

2. **A)** In a school

   B) In an office

   C) In a hospital

   D) In a taxi

3. **A)** Susie frequently misses class.

   B) Susie misses class only when she is sick.

   C) Susie is almost always sick.

   D) Susie doesn't like the class.

4. **A)** The woman lives in Ohio.

   B) The man lives in Ohio.

   C) The man does not think about appropriate clothes for the weather.

   D) Both the man and the woman are concerned about fashionable clothes.

All Work and No Play Makes Jack a Dull Boy

In this unit you will practice: reduced word stress in phrases

Before you begin: Discuss the following questions with your classmates.

◆ Look at the title. What do you think it means?

◆ Do you think both people in the picture want to study?

A. **Read the questions. Then listen to the conversation and answer them.**

1. What is Khareem doing?

2. What day is it?

3. Where are Steve and Jack going?

4. Why does Steve say "All work and no play makes Jack a dull boy"?

5. Do you think that Khareem will go with them?

B. Just as words have stressed and unstressed syllables, phrases have stressed and unstressed words. Which words in this sentence receive less stress than the others?

> A's are better than B's.

Listen to the phrases and underline the unstressed words.

1. give him a book
2. all work and no play
3. where am I going?
4. as good as gold
5. he would do it
6. she came for it
7. you can study
8. I need to study
9. but why not?
10. I said that I did it
11. it's from me
12. come at ten
13. give her the book
14. it was terrible
15. how do they do it
16. send them by mail
17. I need some paper
18. some men are good

Now listen to the phrases again and repeat them.

The unstressed forms of the words above are called the "weak forms." These words sound different when they are pronounced alone. This form is called the "strong form." Listen to the strong form of the unstressed words above and note the difference.

Remember that your pronunciation will not be correct if you use the strong form when you should use the weak form. You may think it is clearer, but Americans may actually find it more difficult to understand you.

C. Dictation. Listen to the dictation first. Then listen and write the sentences. Finally, listen and check your work.

1. _____
2. _____
3. _____
4. _____
5. _____

D. Listen to the chant. Then repeat it line by line.

Balance

All work and no play makes Jack a dull boy,
You can study if you want,
Don't have to be coy,
Just remember that good grades are not life's only joy.

You need to do some work,
You need to do some play,
You need to keep them in balance,
To live another day.

E. Talking Together. Follow the instructions below.

STUDENT A: You are a very busy person. Complete the timetable below with as many work-related activities as you can think of. Your partner is going to ask you to go to the movies. Let him or her know that you can't go because you have too much work.

STUDENT B: Try to convince your partner to go to the movies with you on Friday or Saturday night.

	Friday	Saturday
9–12		
1–3		
4–6		
7–9		
10–12		

F. Looking Ahead to the TOEFL® TEST

Listen to the conversation. Then someone will ask you a question. Read the four choices and circle the one that best answers the question.

1. **A)** She doesn't want to see the play.

   B) She already saw the play.

   C) She wants to see the play.

   D) She is going to see the play.

2. **A)** Bill is senseless.

   B) That the woman is breathless.

   C) It's not worth talking to Bill.

   D) Bill doesn't understand English.

3. **A)** It's fine.

   B) Not all of them.

   C) She can't.

   D) She doesn't have many cats.

4. **A)** The woman studied.

   B) The woman didn't study.

   C) The woman got the answer right.

   D) The woman didn't fail the test.

unit 18

Curiosity Killed the Cat

In this unit you will practice: adding and changing syllable stress

Before you begin: Discuss the following questions with your classmates.

♦ Why do you think we say "Curiosity killed the cat" rather than "Curiosity killed the dog"?

♦ What do you think the woman in this picture is curious about?

A. **Read the questions. Then listen to the conversation and answer them.**

1. What does Margie want to know?

2. Ralph says two things about cats. What are they? What do they mean?

3. What's in the box?

4. Who is going to get the box and why?

B. Some words change stress when a suffix is added. Listen to these pairs of words and mark the stressed syllables.

EXAMPLE: <u>his</u>tory   his<u>tor</u>ical

administer	administration	agriculture	agricultural
argument	argumentative	biology	biological
certify	certificate	curious	curiosity
economics	economist	electricity	electrical
examine	examination	geology	geological
grammar	grammarian	library	librarian
personal	personality	photo	photographer
register	registration	sympathy	sympathetic
technology	technological	utility	utilitarian

Listen and repeat the pairs of words.

C. Some words change their stress when they change part of speech, even if they do not add a suffix. Listen to these sentences and mark the stress in the under-lined word.

1. He <u>conducts</u> himself very well.
2. His <u>conduct</u> is excellent.

3. I broke the <u>record</u>.
4. Who is going to <u>record</u> the dialogue?

5. There is a big <u>contrast</u> between city and country life.
6. The teacher asked us to <u>contrast</u> the philosophies.

7. Is she going to <u>present</u> the award?
8. I need to know who was <u>present</u> in class.

9. I'm trying to <u>perfect</u> my invention.
10. Tom has a <u>perfect</u> record.

11. The poem is <u>attributed</u> to Shakespeare.
12. She has many good <u>attributes</u>.

13. He looks like a <u>convict</u>.
14. He was <u>convicted</u> of a serious crime.

D. Listen to the chant. Then say it line by line.

Stressed Out

Librarians work in libraries,
Grammarians study grammar,
To certify for certificates,
Does stress **really** matter?
I'm all confused,
I'm all stressed out,
Please tell me how it can be,
That my sympathetic teacher has no sympathy for me!

E. Pronunciation Bee. Your teacher will divide your class into two teams. He or she will then hold up a card with a word you have studied. The first person on one team has to say the word correctly. If this person can't, he or she must sit down and the first person on the other team has to say the word. In the case of the words that are spelled the same, the teacher will write a sentence with the word and you must say the sentence. The game continues until one team has no more players.

Here are some words your teacher might ask you to pronounce:

argumentative	average	biology	certainly	comfortable
convention	covering	curious	curiosity	difference
economics	economist	electrical	electricity	family
favorite	frightening	grammarian	historical	history
hotel	interesting	laboratory	librarian	library
listener	mathematics	personal	personality	photographer
ridiculous	several	sympathetic	technological	technology
unfortunately	vegetable			

F. Looking Ahead to the TOEFL® TEST

Listen to the conversation. Then someone will ask you a question. Read the four choices and circle the one that best answers the question.

1. **A)** The robbery is solved.

   B) The robber has turned up.

   C) There are no clues.

   D) The robbery was in the daytime.

2. **A)** To a park

   B) To a beach

   C) To the mountains

   D) To a swimming pool

3. **A)** She's jealous too.

   B) She's not jealous.

   C) She would be jealous.

   D) She wouldn't be jealous.

4. **A)** An optometrist

   B) A dentist

   C) A teacher

   D) A psychologist

Don't Give Up

In this unit you will practice: stress in two-word verbs

Before you begin: Discuss the following questions with your classmates.

◆ Have you ever wanted to quit something? Why?

◆ Study the body language of these two people. What do you think they are talking about?

A. **Read the questions. Then listen to the conversation and answer them.**

1. Why is Paolo upset?

2. What does he want to do?

3. What does Carlos suggest?

4. What happened to Paolo's exams?

B. English has many two-word verbs. In two-word verbs the stress is on the second part of the verb. Listen to these phrases. Mark the stressed word.

1. put on your coat
2. come back tomorrow
3. take off your hat
4. throw away the garbage
5. try out the invention
6. turn on the radio
7. don't let me down
8. I'll make it up
9. don't drop out

Listen again and repeat the phrases.

Some two-word verbs can also be nouns and adjectives. Listen and see how the stress changes. Mark the stressed word.

1. it was a put-on
2. a great comeback
3. a perfect takeoff
4. a throw-away line
5. a fair tryout
6. it's a turn-on
7. what a letdown
8. a make-up exam
9. don't be a dropout

Listen again and repeat the phrases.

C. Listen and build up the sentences from right to left. Don't forget to keep the words between the dashes together.

1. She always—looks after—her sister's children—on the weekend.
2. We invited them over—for lunch—on Saturday.
3. I have to—take the slacks back—to the store—on Broad Street.
4. They called off—Monday's meeting—because of—the bad weather.

D. Listen to the chant. Then repeat it line by line.

Bedtime

Clean up the kitchen,
Take out the garbage,
Shut off the TV,
Turn off the light.

Put away your books,
Hang up your clothes,
Let out the cat,
Say good night.

E. Talking Together. Write a conversation with a classmate. Use as many two-word verbs as you can. Which pair of students uses the most?

F. Looking Ahead to the TOEFL® TEST

Listen to the conversation. Then someone will ask you a question. Read the four choices and circle the one that best answers the question.

1. **A)** A typewriter

   B) A piano

   C) A computer

   D) A lock

2. **A)** A waitress

   B) A store clerk

   C) A nurse

   D) A flight attendant

3. **A)** That Greg really wants to continue the relationship

   B) That Greg doesn't really want to continue the relationship

   C) That Greg already broke the engagement

   D) That Greg is already married

4. **A)** Swimming

   B) Basketball

   C) Golf

   D) Boxing

Six of One, Half a Dozen of the Other

In this unit you will practice: numbers

Before you begin: Discuss the following questions with your classmates.

◆ What do you think the title means?

◆ What do you think these people are planning to do?

A. **Listen to the conversation and and write down the numbers you hear.**

B. **Listen and circle the numbers you hear.**

thirty	thirteen	sixty	sixteen	eighty	eighteen
forty	fourteen	seventy	seventeen	ninety	nineteen
fifty	fifteen				

Listen and repeat the numbers.

C. **Dictation. Listen to the sentences and complete them with the numbers that you hear.**

1. It cost _____. So it will be _____ with tax.

2. Ostriches live for about _____ years.

3. The Easter Rebellion in Ireland was in _____.

4. Greyhounds can run _____ kilometers an hour.

5. Vasco da Gama began his second voyage around the world in _____.

6. The tunnel between France and England is _____ km long.

7. There are _____ muscles in the human body.

8. The area of the Sultanate of Oman is _____ square kilometers.

The information above is "number trivia." Think of some more number trivia (you can use information about your country) or look up information in a reference book. Tell a classmate and let him or her write down the numbers.

D. **Listen to the chant and complete it below.**

Numbermania

_____ or _____,

_____ or _____,

_____ or _____,

_____ or more.

_____

_____

_____

My gosh, that should be plenty.

E. **Talking Together. Use the chart to plan a car trip with a friend. Then tell another classmate about it.**

Destination	Miles	Hours	Expenses		
			gas	food	lodging

F. Looking Ahead to the TOEFL® TEST

Listen to the conversation. Then someone will ask you a question. Read the four choices and circle the one that best answers the question.

1. **A)** Who canceled the flight

   B) Which flight was canceled

   C) Who said that the flight was canceled

   D) Why the flight was cancelled

2. **A)** Break some lamps

   B) Four more

   C) Stop for a while

   D) Quit working

3. **A)** The woman made Dan up.

   B) The woman saw Dan.

   C) The woman likes Dan.

   D) The woman had a fight with Dan.

4. **A)** The theater

   B) The movies

   C) A basketball game

   D) Bowling

unit 21

Review

A. **Read the questions. Then listen to the conversation and answer them.**

1. Where does this conversation take place?

2. How much do five stamps cost?

3. What is the problem with the addresses?

4. How many times has the person sent letters to Japan?

5. What does the post office worker suggest?

6. What city are the letters going to?

B. **Listen to these sentences and write the missing words in the blanks.**

1. She _____ give _____ _____ car.

2. Don't forget _____ buy ham _____ cheese.

3. Send _____ a present _____ _____ wedding.

4. Some men _____ good _____ teaching.

5. I said _____ I wanted _____ go.

6. We _____ leave whenever _____ convenient _____ _____.

7. I _____ _____ letter _____ _____ today.

8. She needs _____ work by tomorrow _____ _____ latest.

9. It _____ _____ terrible storm _____ caused millions _____ dollars _____ damage.

10. How _____ _____ go _____ school _____ _____ _____ full-time job _____ _____ same time?

C. Listen to the words. Write them in the correct columns.

1st syllable stress	2nd syllable stress	3rd syllable stress	4th syllable stress

D. Dictation. Listen to the dictation first. Then listen and write the sentences. Finally, listen and check your work.

_____

_____

_____

_____

_____

E. Talking Together. Look at the words and phrases below. With your partner, make up a conversation using at least ten of them.

biological	favorite	personal
chocolate	forty	a record
comfortable	history	several
to convict	interesting	thirteen
a dropout	librarian	to throw away
examination	to make up the exam	to turn on the light
family	a perfect takeoff	

F. Looking Ahead to the TOEFL® TEST

Listen to the conversation. Then someone will ask you a question. Read the four choices and circle the one that best answers the question.

1. **A)** She goes to Harvard.

   B) She's an excellent student.

   C) She's not a good student.

   D) She would like to go to Harvard.

2. **A)** Perhaps she can use the program.

   B) The whole program is fine.

   C) The woman is right.

   D) She needs to start again.

3. **A)** He doesn't work very much.

   B) He doesn't like baseball.

   C) He works hard.

   D) He and Cheryl work together.

4. **A)** He'll make up his mind later.

   B) He's made up his mind already.

   C) He's not going on vacation.

   D) His options are equal.

It Takes Two to Tango

In this unit you will practice: contrastive stress

Before you begin: Discuss the following questions with your classmates.

◆ These people are dancing the tango. How would you describe this type of dancing?

◆ What do you think the expression "It takes two to tango" means?

A. **Read the questions. Then listen to the conversation and answer them.**

1. Who had a fight?

2. Why was Rick angry?

3. What does Consuela suggest?

4. What's wrong with the suggestion?

B. **In English, we usually stress the last word or words in a sentence because this is usually the most important information. However, sometimes we stress other words in the sentence when we want to make sure that the listener gets the correct message.**

I won the Spanish prize. (normal stress)

Contrastive Stress

I won the Spanish prize. (Joe didn't win; I did.)
I *won* the Spanish prize. (I didn't lose.)
I won *the* Spanish prize. (the most important one)
I won the *Spanish* prize. (not French or German)

Listen to these sentences and circle the information that the speaker thinks is the most important.

1. We're going to have the math exam on Tuesday.

2. We're going to have the math exam on Tuesday.

3. We're going to have the math exam on Tuesday.

4. We're going to have the math exam on Tuesday.

Listen and repeat the sentences.

C. **Now say these sentences with the correct stress to give the messages in parentheses.**

1. Reiko is coming to supper tomorrow. (a. not today) (b. not Lucy)

2. President Kennedy was killed in 1963. (a. not 1964) (b. not elected)

3. Surfing isn't allowed on this beach. (a. Swimming is.) (b. It is on others.)

4. Francine had an accident in my car. (a. not hers) (b. not a breakdown)

D. **Listen to the chant and circle the words with contrastive stress. Then listen again and repeat it line by line.**

Hard of Hearing

Do you know where my mother's going?
Your brother?
No, my mother. She's going to France.
Why's she going to a dance?
Not a dance, France. She's going to fly.
Oh, it's nice there in July.
Not July. Fly. She's going by plane.
But she can't go by train.
Not by train. By . . . never mind.

E. **Talking Together. Follow the instructions below.**

STUDENT A: You are telling your classmate what you did yesterday. He or she keeps misunderstanding you. Clarify yourself by using contrastive stress.

STUDENT B: Your classmate is telling you what he or she did yesterday. Repeat the information back to him or her incorrectly.

EXAMPLE:

A: Yesterday I went to the beach with my brother.
B: You went with your *mother*?
A: No, I went with my *brother*.

F. Looking Ahead to the TOEFL® TEST

Listen to the conversation. Then someone will ask you a question. Read the four choices and circle the one that best answers the question.

1. **A)** On the radio

   B) In front of a classroom

   C) On the telephone

   D) On a tape recorder

2. **A)** How to cook

   B) How to do magic

   C) How to get dressed

   D) How to dance

3. **A)** A glass of water

   B) A handkerchief

   C) A coin

   D) A string

4. **A)** A coin

   B) A glass of water

   C) A rubber band

   D) A handkerchief

In One Ear and Out the Other

In this unit you will practice: consonant/ vowel liaisons

Before you begin: Discuss the following questions with your classmates.

◆ What advice might this mother be giving her daughter?

◆ Do you think the daughter is listening to her mother?

A. **Read the questions. Then listen to the conversation and answer them.**

1. What is the relationship between Isabelle, Carrie, and Abigail?

2. Who is angry and why?

3. Who says "In one ear and out the other"? Why?

B. There is often not a clear break between words in phrases. This is especially true when a consonant is followed by a vowel. This connection is often called a "liaison." Listen to these proverbs and underline the liaisons.

> EXAMPLE: His bark is worse than his bite.

1. Seeing is believing.

2. A friend in need is a friend indeed.

3. Sink or swim.

4. All is fair in love and war.

5. A chain is as strong as its weakest link.

Now listen again and repeat the proverbs.

C. Listen and build up the sentences from right to left. Remember to keep the words between the dashes together.

1. Let him—take it—to her.

2. May I—borrow it—tomorrow—please?

3. When did he hear—that rumor—about David—and the girl—in his class?

4. You did it—without—her help.

5. I don't know—how much money—I need—for the trip.

D. Listen to this silly poem.

> Mares eat oats,
> And does eat oats,
> And little lambs eat ivy.
> A kid'll eat ivy too,
> Wouldn't you?

Listen again and mark the liaisons that you hear. Then practice saying the poem.

E. Talking Together. Look at the proverbs in Exercise B. With a classmate, write a conversation illustrating one of them.

F. Looking Ahead to the TOEFL® TEST

Listen to the tape. Then someone will ask you a question. Read the four choices and circle the one that best answers the question.

1. **A)** In a classroom

   B) On a tour

   C) In a museum

   D) In a model home

2. **A)** Sit on the furniture

   B) Eat

   C) Ask questions

   D) Smoke outside

3. **A)** More than 100 years old

   B) Less than 20 years old

   C) About 200 years old

   D) Less than 100 years old

4. **A)** France

   B) Italy

   C) England

   D) United States

Don't Put Off Until Tomorrow What You Can Do Today

In this unit you will practice: linking with change of consonant

Before you begin: Discuss the following questions with your classmates.

- ◆ Why might this woman be having trouble reading?

- ◆ How often do you get your eyes checked?

A. **Read the questions. Then listen to the radio commercial and answer them.**

1. What is this commercial about?

2. How often should people under 40 have their eyes checked? People over 40?

3. Who paid for the commercial?

4. How does the title of the unit refer to the commercial's message?

B. When two consonants run together in a phrase, one often changes its sound. Listen to each word said separately and then in the phrases. What changes do you hear?

this year	you can	white bird	good boy
have to	good money	bad cold	one cup
nice shoes	where's your	ten men	gone back
did you	not me	one car	bad goat

Listen and repeat the phrases.

Now choose five phrases and write a sentence using each one. Say the sentences to your partner.

C. **Listen to the chant. Then repeat the phrases.**

Conversation Bits

this year	you can	white bird	good boy
have to	good money	bad cold	not me
nice shoes	where's your	ten men	gone back
did you?	that's not funny	one car?	go far

D. **Dictation. Listen to the dictation first. Then listen and write the sentences. Finally, listen and check your work.**

1. _____
2. _____
3. _____
4. _____
5. _____

E. **Talking Together. With a partner, write a radio commercial. Try to use the phrases below. Then say the commercial to your class.**

great buy
good price
fantastic deal

F. Looking Ahead to the TOEFL® TEST

Listen to the tape. Then someone will ask you a question. Read the four choices and circle the one that best answers the question.

1. **A)** On the radio

   B) On the train

   C) In a play

   D) On the street

2. **A)** They are sisters.

   B) They are old friends.

   C) They used to work together.

   D) They are strangers.

3. **A)** Publishing

   B) Real estate

   C) Investing

   D) Advertising

4. **A)** Lend money

   B) Sell magazines

   C) Sell advice

   D) Give credit cards

Honesty Is the Best Policy

In this unit you will practice: linking with disappearing consonants

Before you begin: Discuss the following questions with your classmates.

◆ The man in this picture is interviewing for a job. What can he do to make a good impression on the interviewer?

◆ What shouldn't you do or say at a job interview? Why?

A. Read the questions. Then listen to the conversation and answer them.

1. Where is Ben going in the afternoon?

2. How does he feel? Why?

3. What does Tina suggest?

4. Why did Ben get fired?

B. Sometimes when there are two consonants together in a phrase, the first one disappears. This most often happens when the first consonant is *t*. Listen to these phrases.

next month	white bear	best policy	don't want
didn't tell	worried Tina	left leg	best road
West side	iced tea	soft silk	seemed nice
stuffed turkey	fast bus	lift me	blind mice
first man			

Listen to the phrases and repeat them.

There are some English words in which this change has taken place within the word but the spelling has remained the same. Here are some examples:

grandmother	postman	castle
often	handsome	kindness

Can you think of any others?

C. Listen and build up these sentences. Remember to keep the words between the dashes together.

1. We—were going to go—next month.
2. We drank iced tea—and ate—stuffed turkey.
3. The first man—seemed nice—but he wasn't.
4. We don't want—to cause you—any trouble.
5. He lives—on the West Side—and I live—on the East Side.

D. Listen to the chant. Then repeat it line by line.

Too Full

Roast beef,
Fried chicken,
Stuffed turkey,
Baked ham.

Fresh-baked bread,
Boiled potatoes,
Iced tea,
No more, thanks ma'am.

E. Talking Together. With your partner, write another conversation illustrating the proverb "Honesty is the best policy."

F. Looking Ahead to the TOEFL® TEST

Listen to the conversation. Then someone will ask you a question. Read the four choices and circle the one that best answers the question.

1. **A)** In an office

   B) In a restaurant

   C) In a house

   D) On an airplane

2. **A)** She is his teacher.

   B) She is his friend.

   C) She is his job counselor.

   D) She is his secretary.

3. **A)** A secretary

   B) A salesperson

   C) A typesetter

   D) A journalist

4. **A)** 35

   B) 45

   C) 18

   D) 28

Hear No Evil, See No Evil, Speak No Evil

In this unit you will practice: thought groups

Before you begin: Discuss the following questions with your classmates.

- ◆ What are the monkeys illustrating? Is this good advice?

- ◆ Did you ever report someone's actions to the authorities? What happened? How did you feel?

A. **Read the questions. Then listen to the conversation and answer them.**

1. What did Yoshi's roommate do?

2. What does Yoshi decide to do?

3. What's Dr. Mitchell's phone number?

4. What's Dr. Mitchell's address?

B. When we speak, we divide our speech into thought groups. Thought groups usually go down in tone at the end. Listen to your teacher say this sentence:

Hear no evil, see no evil, speak no evil.

Where does your teacher's voice go down?

Thought groups are easy to hear in numbers. Listen to these sentences and circle the thought groups in the number phrases.

My phone number is 5554537.
My address is 3826 Palm Drive.
My social security number is 098425021.
My credit card number is 614250378494.

Listen to the numbers again and repeat them.

C. Using the correct intonation with thought groups can be very important for comprehension. Listen and circle the phrases that you hear.

1. two week-long trips
   two-week long trips

2. 25-inch nails
   twenty 5-inch nails

3. 5-minute long experiments
   5 minute-long experiments

4. 8-meter wide lots
   8 meter-wide lots

5. 37-cent pencils
   thirty 7-cent pencils

Clauses and phrases are usually thought groups. Listen and circle the thought groups in these sentences.

1. Singapore International Airport, which is my favorite, is located about 15 minutes from downtown.

2. That awful woman is my sister!

3. Wherever he goes, he's mobbed by fans wanting to get his autograph, take his picture, or just touch his clothes.

4. Were those children with you all night?

5. Some animals, such as fish, extract oxygen from the waters of rivers and oceans.

D. Listen to this paragraph. Then practice reading it without any breaks.

> A quarter of the Earth's land surface is covered by mountains over 1,000 meters high. They may be single peaks or form part of a huge mountain range. Mountains affect the world's climate and where and how people live. As the temperature falls by 4 degrees Farenheit every 300 meters up, it becomes more and more difficult for plants and animals to survive on mountain slopes.

E. Talking Together. Complete the table below. Then tell another classmate the information. You can use made-up numbers if you prefer.

	yours	*your classmate's*
address		
phone number		
passport number		
social security number		
credit card number		
student ID number		

F. Looking Ahead to the TOEFL® TEST

Listen to the tape. Then someone will ask you a question. Read the four choices and circle the one that best answers the question.

1. **A)** Communications

   B) Mechanical engineering

   C) Psychology

   D) History

2. **A)** How a telephone works

   B) Morse code

   C) Modern electronic communications

   D) Communications inventions

3. **A)** The telegraph

   B) French engineers

   C) Flag-waving

   D) Pre-electronic communications

4. **A)** Alexander Graham Bell

   B) Samuel Morse

   C) Albert Einstein

   D) Thomas Edison

unit *27*

Variety Is the Spice of Life

In this unit you will practice: intonation in tag questions

Before you begin: Discuss the following questions with your classmates.

◆ What does the title of this unit mean to you?

◆ What are some of the choices that students have to make?

A. **Read the questions. Then listen to the conversation and answer them.**

1. What is the man going to do?

2. Why is the woman surprised?

3. What is he going to study?

4. What has he studied?

B. **Tag questions have two different intonation patterns. One goes up:**

That's yours, isn't it?

This indicates a true question. The speaker doesn't know whether the answer is yes or no.

The other pattern goes down:

That's yours, isn't it?

This is not a true question. The speaker is asking for a confirmation of what he or she already believes.

Listen and draw the intonation patterns for these tag questions.

1. He's smart, isn't he?
2. You've passed, haven't you?
3. Boston's in Canada, isn't it?
4. You need the money, don't you?
5. Today's the 14th, isn't it?

6. They left yesterday, didn't they?
7. He'd stolen it, hadn't he?
8. The course is a lot of work, isn't it?
9. We're still going, aren't we?
10. She's the best, isn't she?

Listen again and repeat the sentences.

C. **Say these tag questions to your partner. Follow the intonation pattern given.**

Student A

1. You went, didn't you? (up)
2. The children don't have class today, do they? (down)
3. He's already bought the cake, hasn't he? (down)
4. She's really sick, isn't she? (up)

Student B

1. You went, didn't you? (down)
2. The children don't have class today, do they? (up)
3. He's already bought the cake, hasn't he? (up)
4. She's really sick, isn't she? (down)

D. **Listen. Then repeat the chant line by line.**

High Anxiety

You passed the test, didn't you?
Tell me, tell me that it's true.
He didn't grade it hard, did he?
You didn't end up with a C?

It was easy, wasn't it?
Tell me or I'll have a fit!
Why don't you speak?
Why can't I know?
You always like to torture me so.

E. **Talking Together. Follow the instructions below.**

STUDENT A: Tell your partner an amazing story. He or she will ask you about it by using tag questions.

STUDENT B: Your partner will tell you an amazing story. Ask him or her questions about it by using tag questions.

EXAMPLE:

A: One day I was walking through a forest and I met a bear.
B: You weren't alone, were you?
A: No, I was with some friends.
B: You all ran away, didn't you?
A: No, we stayed still and stopped talking.

Now change roles.

F. Looking Ahead to the TOEFL® TEST

Listen to the conversation. Then someone will ask you a question. Read the four choices and circle the one that best answers the question.

1. **A)** A store

   B) A university

   C) A hospital

   D) An employment office

2. **A)** A passport

   B) A scholarship

   C) A job

   D) Unemployment

3. **A)** The woman just got a job.

   B) The woman is working more hours.

   C) The woman is not working as much.

   D) The woman just quit her job.

4. **A)** January

   B) December

   C) February

   D) November

unit 28

Review

A. **Read the questions. Then listen to the conversation and answer them.**

1. Who is this conversation between?

2. What is Catherine's problem?

3. Where does she have to go and why?

4. What does Dr. Stevens agree to do?

B. **Listen and mark the intonation in these tag questions.**

1. They've all finished the test, haven't they?

2. He's going to begin the work tomorrow, isn't he?

3. No one was hurt in the crash, were they?

4. You don't have $100 in your pocket, do you?

5. She doesn't look like Madonna, does she?

C. **Listen to the sentences and cross out the sounds that disappear or change.**

1. He lives on the West Side, and I live on the South Side.

2. We don't want to go without you.

3. He likes fast cars, great clothes, and good food.

4. Where's your soft silk dress?

5. I put only one cup of sugar in the iced tea.

D. **Listen to the dictation first. Then listen and write. Finally, listen and check your work.**

_____

_____

_____

_____

_____

_____

E. **Talking Together. Follow the instructions below.**

STUDENT A: You are a student with a problem. You want to turn an assigment in late. You know that your professor is very strict. Ask him or her for permission to hand it in a few days late. (Remember to think of a good excuse.)

STUDENT B: You are student A's professor. Student A has a problem with his or her semester project. You are normally very strict about work being turned in on time. Listen and decide what to do.

F. Looking Ahead to the TOEFL® TEST

Listen to the tape. Then someone will ask you a question. Read the four choices and circle the one that best answers the question.

1. A) Physics

    B) Philosophy

    C) History

    D) Political science

2. A) Hobbes

    B) Locke

    C) Berkely

    D) Rousseau

3. A) 400–500 years ago

    B) 1,000 years ago

    C) 100 years ago

    D) 300–400 years ago

4. A) He didn't sleep in a bed.

    B) He sang in his sleep.

    C) He worked in bed.

    D) He rarely slept.

Appendix

Pronunciation Tools

A. Mouth Diagrams. These diagrams show tongue and lip positions. Sounds which have the same tongue and lip positions differ in other ways such as manner of articulation, voicing and aspiration. The presence or absence of voicing is indicated in voiced/voiceless pairs.

1. /l/ /n/ /t/ (voiceless)
   /d/ (voiced)
   Examples: lip, pill, not, can,
   tin, sent, do, did

2. /r/
   Examples: run, tar

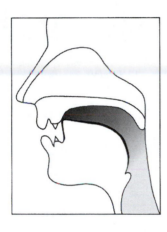
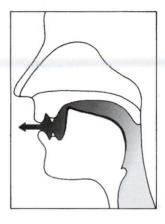

3. /θ/ (voiceless)
   /ð/ (voiced)
   Examples: thin, smooth, the,
   soothe

4. /s/ (voiceless)
   /z/ (voiced)
   Examples: Sue, boss, zoo, knees

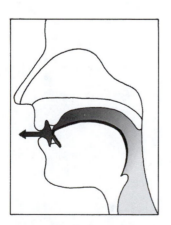
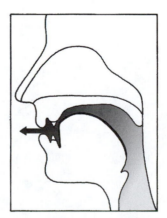

B. Vowel Chart

The Vowel Chart

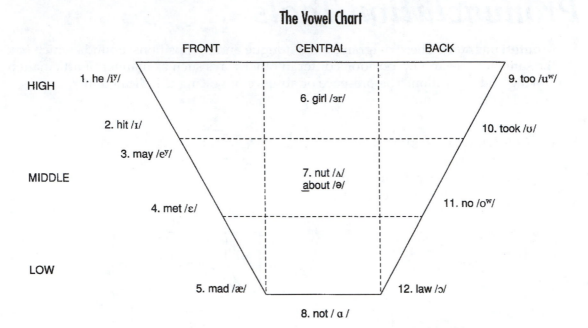

Credits

Photography

All photographs by Jonathan Stark with the exception of:

p. 13   Katrina Thomas/Photo Researchers, Inc.
p. 17   Michael Lajoie
p. 28   Patrick Montagne/Photo Researchers, Inc.
p. 36   AP/Wide World Photos
p. 64   Michael Lajoie
p. 77   Jeffrey Dunn/The Picture Cube